NAISSANCES / BIRTHS

Scripta Humanistica

Directed by
BRUNO M. DAMIANI
The Catholic University of America

ADVISORY BOARD

NAISSANCES / BIRTHS

Jules Supervielle / Philip Cranston

A Bilingual Edition

Scripta Humanistica

86

Library of Congress Cataloging-in-Publication Data

Supervielle, Jules, 1884-1960.
   {Naissances. English & French}
   Naissances = Births : a bilingual edition / Jules Supervielle,
Philip Cranston.
      p.   cm. -- (Scripta Humanistica ; 86)
   French and English on opposite pages.
   Includes the text of En songeant à un art poétique in French
and English.
   ISBN 0-916379-92-2 : $35.00. -- ISBN 0-916379-92-2
   I. Cranston, Philip. II. Supervielle, Jules, 1884-1960. En
songeant à un art poétique. English & French. 1992. III. Title.
IV. Title: Births. V. Series: Scripta Humanistica (Series) ; 86.
PQ2637.U6N313   1992
841'0912--dc20   91-48125
                                                     CIP

Publisher and Distributor:
SCRIPTA HUMANISTICA
1383 Kersey Lane
Potomac, Maryland 20854 U.S.A.

Printed in the United States of America
Imprimé aux Etats-Unis d'Amérique

A la mémoire de Pilar Supervielle

Le Petit Chevalier: Supervielle in 1885

Ni ton cheval ni ton silence
Ni même en moi ton souvenir

(Photo, courtesy of Denise Bertaux-Supervielle)

CONTENTS

POÈMES DE NOVEMBRE
NOVEMBER POEMS

NOUVEAUX POÈMES DE GUANAMIRU
NEW POEMS BY GUANAMIRU

TRANSLATOR'S NOTE

I translate Supervielle because he feels comfortable, familiar. In many ways he is kith and kin, a spiritual brother, cousin, great-uncle, "père nourricier" (as he himself once said of Jules Laforgue)--"un ami inconnu" whom I discovered more than 30 years ago and recognized at once, despite our different continents and cultures.

In a recent interview (*Translation Review* 26, 1988), Burton Raffel--the translator of *Beowulf, Sir Gawain and the Green Knight, Yvain,* and Rabelais--says he translates "only where [he sees] a perceived need"--specifically excluding from the area of need modern French, a language he knows well. "There are plenty of people who also know French, plenty of fine and very active translators." I perceive needs differently and would translate Supervielle even if everyone in the world were able to read French. My need--and pleasure--and agony (translation is also a masochistic enterprise) is to understand, to experience, to appropriate or, rather, share a work of art, to make it partly mine--part of me. If others can enjoy or profit from what I have done essentially for myself, *tant mieux!* I have published, or tried to publish, few of my translations. Their main purpose is served long before they risk smelling printer's ink or staring out of a computer's screen (a thousand points of light?). I let them lie in a drawer or stand on the shelf in file folders and notebooks, always

1

promising myself another bout with them--weeks, months, years, decades down the line. Or to borrow an image from Supervielle: "I come from a family of humble watchmakers, who worked their whole life long, eyes glued to a magnifying glass. The least little springs and wheels must be in place for the poem to set itself in motion."

For it is in the very nature of translation--in its exponentially proliferating potential variability--that a translation is never really done--only (as betters have said before me) abandoned. I have versions begun 40 and more years ago, very much in the yellow leaf but still patiently waiting, waiting to be cured--reclaimed--or laid away again. Each time, they encounter a slightly, or more than slightly, changed me, able perhaps to see what I could not see before or blind to what I once saw. Progress is not necessarily a concomitant of passing time, and deadlines may sharpen the focus of writers--and their translators. But, more Boileau perhaps than Boileau himself, I listen to his (and Horace's) counsel: "Polissez-le sans cesse et le repolissez." Good advice, if your work is no mere silver-plated gloss.

I translate Supervielle, but why *Naissances*? In the late 50s, I had translated two or three short poems from this volume but, over the years, had directed my attention to Supervielle's major works: *Gravitations*, *Le Forçat innocent*, *Les Amis inconnus* and *La Fable du monde*, the four remarkable collections which, from 1925 to 1938, marked out the four corners of his poetic universe and placed him (squarely) in the pantheon of great 20th century French poets.

Naissances, published in January 1951 (the month of Supervielle's 67th birthday)--a mere 76 pages, 25 texts--seems almost an afterthought, an appendix to the Superviellian canon. And yet, despite its modest dimensions, it can serve as an epitome--a sampling and a summing-up--of much that is fascinating in his entire *oeuvre*. It contains poems short

and long (4 to 79 lines; poems of over 30 lines are long--for Supervielle); poems in traditional meter and stanzas (chiefly, quatrains), rhymed, assonated, blank; poems in free verse; prose; lyric poems, dramatic poems (constructed entirely of dialogue), narrative poems (Supervielle referred to the narrative line as the "épine dorsale," the backbone, of many of his poems, even those essentially lyric).

These texts derive from and express many of his obsessive themes and revolve about many of his *mots-clés*, fixed like magnets or little suns in the heart of the poem: anxiety (*anxiété, angoisse*), distress, guilt, suffering, cruelty; confusion, *gravitations*, loss of center and dispersion (in his outer and inner worlds); depths, descent, vertigo, openings, doors, surprises; memory, metamorphoses, exchanges, interpenetrations, creation by thought (creation of the poem and, through it, of new life); the co-existence and quasi-identity of dream-world and reality, the world of fable; God, gods (within and without), goddesses; births, beginnings, the child, woman, the family, the family of man, love, the joy of creating, the preciousness of being alive and the interrelatedness of all life; the soul; sky, mountain, sea; night, suns (both bright and dark); animals (the Superviellian bestiary counts more than two hundred species and subspecies): dog, bull, tiger, sheep, horse, horseback riding (*chevauchée, cavalerie*), birds, flight, fish--and all sorts of inner monsters (tamed and untamed); trees, flowers; heart (with its *intermittences*, its irregular beat), blood; hand, face, the face of the mother he never knew; exile, old age, secrets, silence, statues, stone, the approach of death, the dead, his dead mother.

Ironically, *Naissances* has as much to do with death as with birth--but death tamed (*apprivoisée*), acclimated, "brought up to human temperature" and defanged. Supervielle, in his mid-sixties as he wrote many of these poems, was more and more afflicted by his lifelong chronic tachycardia, asthma,

3

neurasthenia, insomnia. Very much *le malade* (the patient), he keeps his fears at bay with humor, affirmations and acts of creation, with conversations and other exchanges with the dead, gently rubbing at and blurring the boundaries between life and death. Choosing everyday words--"Mots pour tenir compagnie / Lorsque l'on n'est plus en vie" ("Words to keep company by / For those no longer alive")--he creates an ambiguous realm. "Les mots les plus retors désarment sous ma plume, / Même le mot vieillard redoutable entre tous" ("The craftiest words surrender to my pen, / Even the words 'old man' most dreadful of all"), he says in "Nouveaux Poèmes de Guanamiru," the last avatar of his South American self and the fabulous hero of his first novel, *L'Homme de la pampa*, the prose work in which, paradoxically, Supervielle finally found his way and voice as a poet and was liberated to write his first masterpiece, *Gravitations*.

With all that, *Naissances* also includes a significant prose text, "En songeant à un art poétique," Supervielle's *ars poetica*, an essential document for understanding his conception of poetry and his vision; his processes and procedures as a poet.

Translation Review editor Rainer Schulte writes: "It is rare that a poet [as opposed to a professional translator] will take on the translation of an entire book, since this would involve the translation of poems that the poet-translator might consider weak or poems that are foreign to the the nature of her/his own sensibility" (*T.R.* 26). But despite this implied caveat, it seemed to me worthwhile to attempt all of *Naissances*. Even the distinctly minor poems belong to a pattern and a larger whole, which, I think, it is important to reproduce. And although, like Burton Raffel, I find it "infinitely harder to translate prose than to translate poetry" and have put off to the end confronting the two prose texts of *Naissances*, I feel they too should be included. (The second

4

of these was made more attractive by a charming little poem set like a gem in the circle of its text.)

I have read *ad nauseam* the same article about the art or craft of translation--and I have written it myself two or three times. Dryden said it all, 300 years ago: metaphrase (or literal translation), paraphrase, imitation: the three available options as far back as cultures and languages have rubbed up against and polished each other. Translators try, or do not try, to be literal (with all the choices that implies), prize different aspects of their original, and take comfort in the ancient principle of Compensation: what I take away here, I will render somewhere else. The temptation is, of course, to render ten-fold. A translation may become a launchpad for all sorts of creative flights. Strictly, when applying this principle (i.e., when padding or cutting), one should conform to the spirit of the original author as expressed in his other related works, adhering to his vocabulary, making use of his characteristic techniques, his obsessive images and metaphors.

Translators may speak of their art in much the same way, but they never produce the same translation. We do what we can, and each of us is limited in different ways. What we must try to do, I believe (and here I paraphrase Richard Howard in his Introduction to *Flowers of Evil*), is to keep the poem "suspended" on the tightrope of artifice. The translation must have the tension of art (and artifice)--the same kind or kinds of tension and, if possible, to the same degree as the original. On the c(h)ords of artifice we must find fitting registers and try to strike the right notes.

For me the aspect of the original which I most prize and seek to render--to find an equivalent for--is the movement of the poem: its pauses, its silences, its stops and starts, its balancing of elements--its breathing: its life on the page and in the human voice.

Free verse is, of course, less demanding than formal. Of the translation of free verse someone once said: "It's like shooting fish in a barrel." But every poem poses its own set of challenges and I have frequently found traditional verse less difficult than free, as, in turn, free verse is less difficult than prose!

I observe no fixed general principles of translation; each poem leads me down its own lily path--or path of thorns. French alexandrines do, mostly, become English iambic pentameters (equivalent levels of prosodic formality in the two languages), but they may also wander into anapaestic tetrameters etc.: it often depends on the subject matter and tone of the original. An occasional hexameter mixed in with the pentameters, an anapaest or dactyl with the iambs, help to bridge the distance between French and English versification. In my versions, I have made frequent use of half- (or slant-) rhyme--as does Supervielle--but not always at the same point in a text, according myself the same freedom, as translator, as the poet in his original: "[des] vers blancs qui riment quand la rime vient à moi" ("blank verses which rhyme when a rhyme occurs to me"), he says in his "Art poétique."

For the rest, I have tried to keep to Supervielle's simplicity in language and structure ("les mots de tous les jours"), his sincerity of tone ("le ton réel"), his transparency ("surface limpide," "mystère dans les profondeurs"), his *sagesse* and his humanity--alongside his familiarity, his humor and mischievous playfulness: all the registers and as many of the harmonics as I could manage.

A good translation is the result of hard work, strict discipline and endless patience; but, like a good original poem, it is still a chance and a miracle. Hard work, discipline, patience, a firm theoretical basis and total commitment don't always pay off.

I translate Supervielle (and a number of other kindred spirits) for the sheer pleasure, the sheer torment. It is a challenge, a *gageure*, a bet I certainly cannot finally win (the original text holds all the cards). But there is always the excitement of the game. And the stakes are high--paid in the coin of the realm: the realm of poetry, the realms of gold. The pleasure of holding, weighing, counting out that specie is enough--even if I have failed, by hook or by crook, to make it my own, to play the poet's *double*, to become--rare ambition!--his *alter ego*. Or, to return to the metaphor of Supervielle's title: although most of these births may be miscarriages, a few may survive--or, at least, engender some new poem of mine or of others.

*

"Voici Pilar, elle m'apaise, ses yeux déplacent le mystère"
("Here is Pilar, she calms me, her eyes displace mystery")
("Apparition," *Gravitations*)

"A Pilar, pour la remercier de m'être si chère"
("For Pilar, to thank her for being so dear to me")
(Dedication to *La Fable du monde*)

In late spring 1964, near the end of a two year stay in Paris, I finally took pen and courage in hand and wrote to Pilar Supervielle. I had been translating Supervielle since 1957 or 1958 (at this late date, how be certain?--it feels as though I have been translating Supervielle all my life), and in April 1960, a month before the poet's death, I had presented a selection of Supervielle poems in translation on Berkeley (California) radio station KPFA. But I had hesitated to intrude upon the privacy of the poet's family. A photo I had taken, during the 1964 Easter break, of Supervielle's grave at Oloron-Sainte-Marie (city of his ancestors in the French Pyrenees), with its rough-hewn footstone

inscribed "Ce doit être ici le relais / Où l'âme change de chevaux" ("This must be the relay / Where the soul changes horses"), provided the occasion. That, and a few memorial verses of my own inscribed on the verso.

I need not have waited so long. Pilar's response was immediate, generous, open-hearted: "Your letter touched me deeply. . . . How happy my husband would have been to know you; I sense so many affinities between you." Before my wife and I left for America in August, Pilar invited us to dinner at 15, quai Louis Blériot (Supervielle's last Paris residence), and there we met Supervielle's oldest daughter, Denise, with her husband, the Sorbonne Germanist, Pierre Bertaux. In September, Pilar wrote to us (now in California): "Your charming letter gave me great pleasure. It is surely sincere, for your arrival at my doorstep inspired reciprocal feelings in me. And for good reason: you have my husband's silhouette, his bearing, his reserve, your silence was his, and your timidity. Your wife, my face when I was younger ('mon visage d'antan'), my hairdo. A reincarnation almost." And, after telling us of her husband's hatred of ostentation, his generosity, his *droiture* (uprightness, decency), his friendships, his love for her and for their children (especially their daughters), his fondness for travel, movies, television (for the distraction, the escape, they provided from obsessive preoccupations), the pleasure he took in reciting his poems in public--preferably a small public ("and he knew he recited them very well"), his fragile health, his preoccupation with death, Pilar concludes: "Forgive this disorganized letter; I would have liked to speak of the Poet in words worthy of him and of you--but that I must leave to you: you will know how to do it."

Alas, I have not known how to do it; --at least, have not done it, until now. Pilar saw my first published Supervielle translations in my collection, *Time of the Sun* (1968), which

takes its title from the first line of a Supervielle poem: "Un jour. . . nous dirons: 'C'était le temps du soleil'" ("Le Regret de la terre," *Les Amis inconnus*). She wrote to express her (overgenerous) appreciation of my own poems ("mon mari les aurait aimés") and her happiness that my poetry had "penetrated the translations, permitting them to find new life" in my language. Between 1969 and 1971, there were other letters, other invitations, another dinner at 15, quai Louis Blériot; our friendship deepened.

And then: --silence.

Pilar, I have broken faith with you. I have not kept my promise. It is late. But perhaps not too late? You are not with us to see or to hear. . . and yet, in the Superviellian scheme of things, perhaps yes: "(For) we were there on every hand to watch," say the dead in one of the poems of *Les Amis inconnus*. Let me begin today and redeem the lost years, my long silence.

*

My heartfelt thanks to Denise Bertaux-Supervielle for the permission--and encouragement--she gave me already more than a decade ago to pursue this and other, more ambitious, projects involving the translation of entire volumes of her father's poetry. May the few texts of *Naissances* serve as *prémices*, first fruits, of a richer harvest.

For permission to publish these translations and to reprint *Naissances*, and for ready and generous support: my grateful acknowledgment to Gallimard, publisher of Supervielle's four novels, three collections of short stories, six plays (including a translation of Shakespeare's *As You Like It*), two memoirs, nine major collections of mature poetry (beginning with *Gravitations* in 1925)--and of how many other seminal works and memorable voices of the twentieth century.

Last but far from least, I wish to thank my wife, Mechthild, for her steadfast confidence in me, her unstinting help in every aspect of this enterprise--from the struggle with words and rhythms to the trials and (t)errors of "computerization."

These *BIRTHS*, these many moons
In labor, dear M(id)-Wife,
Are yours as much as mine:
The puny, puling proof
Of my inconstant skill,
Nursed to a fitful life
By your unwavering will.

Breathe on my words unborn,
Breathe through my heart the fire
Of future dawns--and noons.

INSOMNIE

INSOMNIA

INSOMNIE

Chevaliers de la nuit blanche, cavalerie
Sans mémoire qui se concentre et qui s'agite...
On se heurte, on chuchote, on se félicite
Avant de repartir pour massacrer un coeur.
Et comment contenir ces voraces chimères
Antagonistes, sur l'oreiller irrité?
Le sang pousse un tumulte accru dans les artères
Et le coeur s'interroge et feint de s'arrêter.
Le matin saura-t-il demain luire sur terre,
Sur toi-même morceau de nuit épouvanté
D'être à la fois de terre et de ciel et de pluies
D'un passé très lointain que le présent essuie?
Mais où est le présent dans cette obscurité
Au fond de l'insomnie où l'on nie et renie
Et qui nous cherche noise et qui nous calomnie,
Nous verse son acide en flammes dans les yeux
Et de notre bois mort fait un feu furieux.
O souffrance, ô rocher en nous inextricable,
Tu mets en sang la chair et ses tissus secrets
Ou bien tu vas t'asseoir à notre pauvre table
Suçant l'anxiété comme un os de poulet,
Tu t'installes partout où l'on trouve de l'homme
Et tu viens fureter de tes rugueux couteaux

INSOMNIA

Riders of the sleepless night, cavalry
Merging and surging, blank, unmemoried. . .
They jostle, whisper, praise each others' feats,
Then wheel about to massacre a heart.
And how contain these ravening chimeras
Battling upon a pillow vexed and frayed?
The blood provokes a tumult in the veins,
And the heart questions itself, pretends to halt.
Morning tomorrow will it shine again
On earth, on yourself, fragment of night, appalled
To be composed of earth and sky and rains
Of a far-off past the present wipes away?
But where is the present in these murky depths
Of sleeplessness where we abjure, deny,
Which quarrels with us and hurls calumnies,
Which pours its flaming acid in our eyes
And of our dead wood makes a raging fire.
O suffering, o rock in us inextricable,
You bloody the flesh, its secret cells and zones
Or else sit down with us at our poor table
Sucking anxiety like a chicken bone,
You settle in wherever there is man
And with your jaggèd knives you ferret out

Ce qui se fait de triste et de grand sous la peau
Jusqu'à ce que repue enfin on fasse un somme
Et qu'on vous laisse là ouvert comme un tombeau
Qui sent l'humidité suppliante de l'homme.
Qu'un sommeil justicier allège nos paupières
Et nous confie enfin à ces concaves pierres
Qui épousent les corps aux grandes profondeurs.
La chair au bord du cri étouffe son horreur
Et toi, nuit grande ouverte aux marches du silence
Viens nous ensevelir dans ton indifférence,
Guide-nous dans les vestibules du dormeur
Qui n'entend plus son coeur aboyer à la lune
Et monte à bord du songe où l'on devient posthume.
Que s'éteigne tout ce phosphore de nos yeux
Traçant et retraçant ses cercles soupçonneux!
Dormir! ne plus savoir ce qu'on nomme la Terre,
Ce cercle de sommeil est le frère des cieux?
J'ignore ces pays et ces à peine lieux,
Cette géographie étrange et salutaire
Où vont couler sans fin les rêves, leurs rivières,
Où la métamorphose affine ses pinceaux
Sous un ciel de passage et toujours jouvenceau
Le long de l'océan où se défait la vie
Après sa méandreuse, aveuglante insomnie.

All that is sad and noble beneath the skin
Till, sated at last, turning and drowsing off,
You leave us there, laid open like a tomb
Smelling of mankind's supplicating dampness.
May a rectifying slumber lighten our lids,
At last commit us to those hollowed stones
That at great depths take on our bodies' forms.
Flesh verging on a cry chokes back its horror
And you, night wide open to the steps of silence
Come bury us in your indifference,
Guide us into the hallways of the sleeper
Who no longer hears his heart bay at the moon
And climbs aboard the dream that drifts past death.
Let all this phosph'rous of our eyes die out
Tracing, retracing its distrustful circles!
To sleep! no more to know what men call Earth,
This circle of sleep is it the heavens' brother?
I do not know these lands, these barely places,
This strange geography so salutary
Where dreams flow, endless, with their tributaries,
Where metamorphosis refines its brushes
Under a migratory sky forever young
Along the ocean where life comes undone
After its winding, blinding sleepless night.

MÉTAMORPHOSES

METAMORPHOSES

CE PUR ENFANT

Ce pur enfant, rose de chasteté,
Qu'a-t-il à voir avec la volupté?
Et fallait-il qu'en luxe d'innocence
Allât finir la fureur de nos sens?

Dorénavant en cette neuve chair
Se débattra notre amoureux mystère?
Après nous avoir pris le coeur d'assaut
L'amour se change en l'hôte d'un berceau,

En petits poings fermés, en courtes cuisses,
En ventre rond sans aucune malice
Et nous restons tous deux à regarder
Notre secret si mal, si bien gardé.

PURE CHILD

Pure child, rose-blush of chastity,
Is this our sensuality?
Such luxury of innocence commences
With the frenzy of our senses?

Henceforward in this newborn flesh
Will our love's mystery strive afresh?
After having stormed our breast
Love turns into a cradle's guest--

To small clenched fists, to legs upbent,
To chubby tummy (no harm meant),
And we look on--no need to tell--
Our ill-kept secret kept so well.

NAISSANCE D'UN PALMIER

L'âme invisible et tout de même lourde
On se veut palme en son intimité,
Et l'on est un désir aux belles courbes,
Fourmillement de pressantes fiertés,
On ne peut plus dissimuler sa face
On va bondir dans sa réalité
Et tout d'un coup emplissant son espace
Fuse un palmier ivre de vérité,
Le tronc bien pris de taille et le bouquet
Illuminé d'un luxe perspicace,
Bien accroché de racines voraces
Il vibre encor de sa témérité
Quand un oiseau vérifiant la place
Y fait son nid et sa félicité.

BIRTH OF A PALM TREE

With soul invisible yet heavy-burdened,
One wills oneself a palm branch inwardly,
And now we are desire with lovely curves,
A teeming forth of urgent pride and faith,
And now we can no longer hide our face
And we must leap to our reality
And all at once filling its space
A palm bursts forth made drunk with sudden truth,
Long-stemmed and elegant, its crown ablaze
With luxuries of shrewd profusion,
Hooked tightly to the earth by greedy roots,
Still quiv'ring at its own temerity--
When a stray bird, confirming its place,
Chooses it for her nest and her felicity.

Sort-il de moi ce chien avec sa langue altière
Effaré comme s'il improvisait la Terre,
Est-ce encore un peu moi qui se couche à mes pieds
Et regarde parfois si je suis satisfait
        De lui et de moi-même
        Et de tout ce que j'aime?

Je l'entends respirer, heureux et respectable,
Ce moi plus malchanceux coupé de ses vocables.
Il cherche une sortie à tant de sentiments
Et de confusion qu'il en est haletant.
        Ne lui disons plus rien
        Laissons-le être chien.

From me? this dog with his haughty tongue--strange birth
Dumbfounded as if improvising Earth?
Still partly me, he's crouching at my feet
And looking to see if I am satisfied
      With him--below, with me--above,
      With all I love?

I hear him breathing, happy and dignified,
This more unlucky me, cut off from his words.
He's hunting for ways out of so much feeling,
So much confusion that it leaves him panting.
      An end to this monologue,
      Let him be dog.

La rose où vous deviez en venir aujourd'hui
Après avoir erré dans des zones confuses
Elle ne sait plus rien de vos anciennes ruses,
Naïve, la voilà comme une fleur qui luit,
Sans honte de montrer ses épines fidèles
Dont elle ne rougit pas plus que son modèle.
Soyez rose, si Dieu nous regarde à regret
C'est que nous violons ses lois et son secret
Et qu'ayant décelé votre métamorphose
On voit s'interroger sur pied toutes les roses.
Sachez, roses, que vos destins sont accomplis.
Ne cache pas qui veut une femme en ses plis.

The rose you were to end up as, today,
After long wandering through twilight zones
What does she know of tricks you used to play,
Naïve, she stands there like a flower that shines,
And unashamed displays her faithful thorns
Which, like her model, she's not blushing for.
Well, be a rose, God looks away because
We violate his secret and his laws
And, with your metamorphosis disclosed,
Self-questioning harasses every rose.
Roses, know this, your destiny's fulfilled.
We can't all hide a woman in our folds.

25

FUGITIVE NAISSANCE

Où rien n'était qu'un peu de rose habituel
Mais toujours sur le bord du vertige qui ose,
S'agitant tout d'un coup sous l'immobile ciel
Un enfant se forma dans les ombres moroses.

Ses petits poings serrés sur un restant de nuit,
Les yeux clos pour mieux consentir à la lumière,
Nu sous les lances du soleil et sous ses pierres
Il n'a pour bouclier que le duvet des fruits.

Une longue lionne à la langue qui luit
Et s'approche, s'en vient lui lécher la paupière,
Son poil est radieux où des comètes fuient
Sans fin sous le regard pour toujours se refaire.

L'enfant ouvre les yeux, hasarde leurs pinceaux
Sur ce corps frémissant de bête fabuleuse,
Puis rassemblant les rais des rétines peureuses
S'esquive en un sommeil qui l'efface à nouveau.

Et la bête léchant ce vide qui respire
Se fige et tarde à se changer en souvenir.

FUGITIVE BIRTH

Where all there was was just the usual pink
But always verging on some dizzying brink,
Suddenly stirring beneath a sky stock-still
A child took shape down in the sullen dark.

His small fists clench a remnant of the night,
Eyes closed, the better to accept the light,
Naked beneath the sun's spears and its stones,
His only shield the soft down of a fruit.

A long lioness, with luminous tongue
Advancing, comes and licks his lids,
Her hair is radiant where bright comets plunge
By, endlessly, now in, now out of sight.

The child opens his eyes, ventures their brushes
Upon that fabulous beast's long quivering frame,
Then gathering in the retina's shy rays
Slips gently off, erased again by sleep.

And the beast licking at this breathing void
Freezes and for awhile forgets to change
                Into a memory.

VISION

Votre visage, seul, à travers la froidure,
M'arrive après avoir fait voyage dans l'air,
Mais comment a-t-il fait pour franchir la nuit dure,
Sans le corps traversant le glacial désert.

Négligente du siècle et de l'espace, armés
Toujours de pied en cap et qui tuent sans faiblesse.
Visage, vous venez, du givre dans vos tresses,
Et cet oubli du monde où vous me souriez!

Vous qui m'apparaissez sans espoir, sans caresses,
Que faire l'un de l'autre, ô courage, ô détresse!

Amour, toi qui nous suis des yeux et qui nous loges,
Tu fais de notre coeur un fruit chéri des dieux,
Ils aiment les assauts des couples anxieux
Contemplant nos élans tronqués qu'ils interrogent.

La brûlure des sens les enivre de vin,
Leurs yeux brillent, ils font un tapage hautain
Et se frappant la cuisse à voir que nous transportent
Nos sombres coeurs fiévreux s'ouvrant comme une porte

Pour que puisse tomber sur le bord du chemin
Une tête roulant comme tête de morte.

VISION

Your face, alone, across the cold and blight,
Reaches me from its journey through the skies.
How did it come to leap the rigid night
And, bodiless, pass through that desert of ice.

You heedless of time and space, armed in their pride
From head to foot and killing without fail.
O face, you come with hoar-frost in your braids,
Forgetful of the world to which you smile!

O you, who seem so hopeless, uncaressed,
What can we do? O courage, O distress!

Love, who pursue us with possessive eyes,
You make our heart a fruit dear to the gods,
They love the bouts of anxious couples, watching
And questioning our mutilated flights.

Our burning senses make them drunk with wine,
They make a haughty hubbub, their eyes shine,
They slap their thighs to see us so transported
By dark feverish hearts that open like a door

That there may fall beside the road
A head that rolls like some dead woman's head.

COLLOQUE

Par-dessus notre tête
Les dieux qui nous habitent
Echangent des paroles
En allongeant le cou.
Et nous les entendons dire distinctement
Nos noms et nos prénoms comme si nous étions
Déjà morts et sans goût pour toute la nature
Qui s'échelonne sans sortir du grand silence
Dont nous faisons partie.
Ils nous jugent, nous pèsent,
Piétinent nos nuances
Et hurlent nos secrets
Puis soudain les voilà pires que des statues
Immobiles et froids comme des ponts de fer
Sous lesquels nous passons,
Honteux d'être si nus
Et si désabusés,
Mais encore un peu fiers
Que loin derrière nous rayonne la montagne
Et devant nous la mer.

COLLOQUY

Over our heads
The gods who dwell in us
Bandy their words
Craning their necks.
And we hear them say distinctly
Our names, our last names first, as if we were
Already dead, with no taste left for nature
Spaced out inside the boundaries of silence
To which we too belong.
They judge us, weigh us,
Stamp out our shades of difference
And shout our deepest secrets
Then, worse than statues, stand
Motionless and cold like iron bridges
Under which we pass,
Ashamed to be so naked
And so disabused
Yet still a little proud
That far behind us shines the mountain,
In front of us the sea.

LE SANG

Mon sang a pris mon coeur pour sa montagne
Et se déverse avec un bruit léger
Dans cette plaine humaine et sans vergers
Qui fait le corps cherchant une compagne,

Le sang ne coule pas pour lui tout seul
Ou le voilà blafard comme un linceul,
Aveugle, il aime au loin chercher fortune
N'y voyant clair que pour blondes et brunes.

Autour de lui et ne se trompant pas
Il vise au loin les sources de la vie,
Et toujours prêt aux plus tendres combats
Va dévalant vers les rives ravies.

THE BLOOD

My blood has made a mountain of my heart
And flowing with a gentle sound
Descends into that orchardless and human ground
Which is the body searching for a mate,

Not for itself alone the blood flows down
Or it grows paler than a shroud,
Blind, it would seek its fortune far off, --best
Seeing the light for blonds and for brunettes.

On every side, with sense that never errs,
It seeks the far-off springs of life,
And always ready for the tenderest strife,
Goes rushing downwards towards the ravished shores.

Elle lève les yeux et la brise s'arrête,
Elle baisse les yeux, la campagne s'étend,
Elle tourne la tête une rose se prend
Au piège et la voilà qui tourne aussi la tête
Et jusqu'à l'horizon rien n'est comme avant.

She lifts her eyes, the breeze stops dead,
She lowers her eyes, the fields stretch out,
She turns her head a rose is caught
In the trap and it too turns its head--
To the edge of the sky this change has spread.

Les golfes aux beaux noms, les collines légères,
En limpide appareil se présentent à moi,
La mer remplit les creux et le ciel bleu reçoit
Ce qui se fait de plus aigu, les passagères
Hirondelles volant de climat en émoi.
Mais serais-je certain d'en avoir vu aucune
Moi qui pense toujours à celles qui viendront
Ou ne seront jamais possibles que de nom,
Puisque je les vois même errantes sous la lune,
Oiseaux de jour perdus dans mes ombres sans fond.

The gulfs with their lovely names, the light-poised hills
In limpid apparel stand before my eyes,
The sea fills in the hollows, the blue skies
Receive the keenest of the keen, the swift swooping
Swallows winging from outer to inner clime.
But how be certain I have seen even one,
I who am thinking always of those to come
Or never to be except in name,
I see them even wanderers under the moon,
Birds of day lost in my bottomless gloom.

LE VISAGE

Pour affronter le ciel il me faut un visage
Qui ne ressemble au mien que par le vif des yeux
Et pour gravir la nuit j'ai besoin de ce bleu,
Ce souvenir du jour et de ma mère sage
Blottie entre mes cils avec tant de pudeur
Que nul ne pense à elle en voyant leur couleur.
Elle sait être moi avec tant de patience
Qu'elle aime à se confondre avec mon ignorance
Et l'on ne songe pas que je ne suis pas seul
A vouloir m'élancer au puits sans fond du ciel.
Pardon de n'avoir su, ô douce ressemblance,
Imiter ta pudeur ni garder ton silence.

THE FACE

To brave the sky I need a face
Unlike my face but for the ardor of its eyes,
To scale the night I need this blue
Token of day and my good mother's gaze
Nestling between my lashes with such reserve
That seeing their color no-one thinks of her.
She can be me with so much patience that
She loves to mingle with my ignorance
And no-one dreams it is not only I
Who long to leap into the sky's deep well.
Forgive me I could never learn, sweet likeness,
To imitate your modesty, your silence.

ACCADEMIA

De la fenêtre d'un musée où le nu des Déesses
Approchait lentement la poitrine des Dieux
Dans la claire maison d'en face, sans dorures,
Je voyais une main qui repassait dans l'ombre
Un linge de nos jours,
Faisant de plus en plus étinceler ce linge
Qui délivrait sa neige à la chaleur du fer
Et la lui confiait en tout aveuglement,
En grande modestie.
Et malgré Tintoret, Véronèse et Titien
Malgré ce qu'animait l'italienne peinture,
Rien ne bougeait entre les cadres inflexibles
Cependant que la main dans la maison d'en face
Passait et repassait le linge et ce beau jour
Que nous vivions ensemble d'une fenêtre à l'autre.
Et rien n'était fictif dans l'humain mouvement
Comme dans ces remous amoureux des peintures
Comme dans ces tableaux de batailles rangées
Où le sang qui coulait
N'était que vermillon et rouge de garance
Au fond d'un sourd passé
Où ne parvenait pas la rumeur citadine.

Venise 49

40

ACCADEMIA

From a museum window where the nakedness of Goddesses
Drew slowly closer to the chests of Gods
In the bright, ungilded house across the way
I watched a hand ironing in the dark
A linen of our days,
Making that linen sparkle more and more
As it released its snow, in utter blindness
Entrusted to the iron and its heat
With great reserve and modesty.
And notwithstanding Tintoretto, Veronese, Titian,
In spite of what Italian painting quickened,
Nothing was stirring between the rigid frames
While the hand in the house across the way
Kept ironing the linen and that radiant day
Which we were living together, one window to the other.
And nothing in our movements was fictitious
Like in those amorous whirls and swirls of art,
Like in those pictures of pitched battles
Where the blood that flowed
Was mere vermilion, madder-red
Deep in a muffled past
Which the din of cities could not reach.

Venice 49

41

POÈMES DE NOVEMBRE

NOVEMBER POEMS

Avec l'âge il était de plus en plus touché
Par la rigidité, les jours sans vent, des arbres,
Et voilà que je suis fasciné par le marbre
Horizontal, en moi de moins en moins caché.

Pins parasols, ouverts en Méditerranée,
Et vous, cyprès mortels, consuls de l'immobile,
Votre silence peut combler beaucoup d'années
Et fera consentir un coeur très difficile.

With age he was affected more and more
By the rigidness, on windless days, of trees,
And here I am held spellbound by this core
Of marble slab inside me hidden less and less.

Umbrella pines, spread wide above the Sea,
And you, death's cypresses, consuls of the still,
Your silence can make up for many years
And will persuade a heart that's hard to please.

Qu'il nous est difficile
De trouver un abri
Même dans notre coeur
Toute la place est prise,
Et toute la chaleur.

How hard it is to find
Shelter and a fire
Even in our heart
There is no room to spare,
There is no warmth.

POSTHUME

Il faudrait donner aux morts des phrases de tous les jours,
Des mots qui facilement vont de nos lèvres à leurs oreilles,
Mots pour tenir compagnie
Lorsque l'on n'est plus en vie.
Aidez-moi, mes amis, les hommes,
Ce n'est pas travail pour un seul,
De ces phrases usagées toutes frottées par les ans
Phrases de vous et de moi aussi bien que de nos pères
Surtout pour les morts à la guerre
Avec leur destin éclaté,
Phrases choisies avec soin
Pour les mettre en confiance.
Rien n'est plus timoré qu'un mort
Sent-il un peu l'air du dehors
Que le voilà tout méfiance,
Phrases qu'il nous faut tenir prêtes
Pour qu'ils s'en frottent un peu les lèvres
Et que les trouvant si belles d'avoir déjà tant servi
Ils éprouvent la petite fièvre
De qui perdit un beau jour la mémoire des ténèbres
Et regarde devant lui.

1934.

POSTHUMOUS

Dead men need to be given everyday words,
Words that easily pass from our lips to their ears,
Words to keep company by
For those no longer alive.
Help me, my friends, fellow humans,
This is no job for one man,
Second-hand words rubbed smooth by the years,
Your words and mine and those of our fathers
Especially for the war-dead
Their destinies shattered,
Words chosen with care
To win their trust.
Nothing more timorous than a dead man--
Just sniffing the out-of-doors
He's filled with instant distrust,
Words we have to keep ready
For them to rub lips against
And, finding them beautiful from so much use,
Feel the slight fever
Of one who one fine day lost all memory of darkness
And looks into the distance.

1934.

J'ai senti que s'ouvrait cette oreille de l'âme
Bien plus fine que l'autre, ayant sienne chaleur,
Elle perçoit toutes nuances du silence
Mais le bruit la rend sourde et l'emplit de rancoeur.

I felt the soul's ear open, keener by far
Than the other, with its own warmth and depth,
It catches every grade and shade of silence
But noise fills it with rancor, makes it deaf.

LA CAGE

Pour se joindre aux oiseaux traçant leurs cercles libres
Il s'obstine à vouloir par les barreaux sortir
     L'oiseau dont les yeux brillent,
Il y plaque à l'envi ses grandes plumes vertes
Se refusant à voir que la cage est ouverte.

1934.

THE CAGE

To join birds circling in the sky
He longs to leave the cage and fly,
   The bird with the burning eyes,
Great green wings against the bars,
He disregards the open door.

1934.

CONSOLATION

Cyprès, vous n'êtes pas arbres de cimetière
Comme vous le pensez
Vous qui montrez le ciel de votre index austère
Sans jamais vous lasser.

Votre zèle touffu, sa sibylline pointe,
De loin comme de près
Sont avec les vivants, l'indifférence est feinte
Qui s'ouvre aux nids secrets.

Ne vous reprochez pas votre métaphysique
Quand vous savez si bien
Par cet unique doigt d'une invisible main
Devenir pathétiques.

CONSOLATION

Cypresses, you are not cemetery trees
    As you suppose
Lifting a finger, sober and severe,
    Unwearied, to the skies.

Your bushy zeal, its sibylline sharp point,
    From near or far--confess!--
Are with the living; that apathy is feigned
    Which opens to secret nests.

Don't blame your metaphysics; bless the real,
    You who understand
By that one finger of an unseen hand
    How to make us feel.

NOUVEAUX POÈMES DE GUANAMIRU

NEW POEMS BY GUANAMIRU

LE MALADE

Trop grand le ciel trop grand je ne sais où me mettre
Trop profond l'océan point de place pour moi
Trop confuse la ville trop claire la campagne.
Je fais ciel, je fais eau, sable de toutes parts,
Ne suis-je pas encore accoutumé à vivre
Suis-je un enfant boudeur qui ne veut plus jouer
Oublié-je que si je tousse
Mes soixante-six ans tousseront avec moi
Et feront avec moi tousser mon univers.
Quand le matin je me réveille
Est-ce que je ne sors pas peu à peu tout entier
De l'an quatre-vingt-quatre, du siècle précédent
Où se font les vieillards?
Mais qui ose parler de vieillards alors que
Les mots les plus retors désarment sous ma plume,
Même le mot vieillard redoutable entre tous
Fait pivoter vers moi un tout neuf tournesol
Brillant comme un jeune homme.
Hache du désespoir taciturne en ma main
Tu te mets à chanter comme fait l'espérance.

THE PATIENT

Too vast the sky too high where can I hide
Too deep the seas too dark no room for me
Too crazed the town too bright the countryside.
And I am sky, am water, sand on every side
And am I still unused to being alive,
A sulking child who won't come out to play,
Do I forget that if I cough
My sixty-six long years will cough with me
And with me make my universe cough too.
Mornings when I wake
Do I not surface bit by bit, intact,
From the year eighteen-hundred-and-eighty-four
Where old men are made?
But who dares speak of old men when
The craftiest words surrender to my pen,
Even the words "old man" most dreadful of all
Make a fresh sunflower, shining like a youth,
Pivot around towards me.
Axe of despair taciturn in my hand
You start to sing like hope for this old man.

PARIS

Que de fois je regardai par la fenêtre en Amérique
Dans l'espoir que vînt à moi un paysage de France
Et c'est Paris qui fait irruption par la croisée
Avec les grandes foulées de Notre-Dame de pierre
Il va traversant les siècles sans avoir à bouger même le petit doigt
Jusqu'à cette bordure frémissante d'écume
Qui forme le moment présent et fait battre notre coeur,
Paris et son brouhaha de chars mérovingiens, ses carrosses dorés,
    ses fiacres, ses automobiles de tous les âges.
Tout ce vacarme étouffé dans l'oeuf par le silence intimidant
    de l'histoire.
Paris avec son pouls parfaitement régulier, sans la moindre
    intermittence
Malgré les catastrophes traversées,
Paris retrouvé par un homme qui te regarde du fond de sa chambre
    et de son coeur
Fidèle à ton ciel où déambulent de grands nuages infidèles
Folle bande versatile qui passerait facilement à l'ennemi.
Chut! le ciel n'a pas de patrie
Et c'est peut-être même ce qui fait sa grandeur,
L'intimité de son accueil à la profondeur inlassable
Où vont et viennent les âmes nues et naissent les ailes des anges.

PARIS

How often I looked out from my window in America
Hoping some landscape might come my way from France
And see! it is Paris bursting in through the casement
With the great stone strides of Notre-Dame,
Paris crossing the centuries, without so much as lifting a finger,
All the way to this narrow margin trembling with foam
Which forms the present and makes our hearts beat,
Paris, its hubbub of Merovingian carts, gilded coaches, carriages,
    automobiles of all ages,
All that uproar nipped in the bud, squashed in the yolk, by the
    intimidating silence of history.
Paris with its perfectly regular pulse, never missing a beat
Despite its catastrophes,
Paris rediscovered by a man who looks at you from the depths
    of his room and his heart
Faithful to your sky where great unfaithful clouds go ambling by,
Flighty and fickle lot perfectly capable of crossing over to the enemy.
Hush! the sky has no country
And that is perhaps what makes for its grandeur.
The intimacy of its welcome, inexhaustibly deep,
Where naked souls come and go and the wings of angels are born.

CONFIANCE

O puissantes montagnes, pendant qu'il en est temps encore
Laissez-nous, les yeux grands ouverts, défier le monde à vos pieds
Avec toute l'autorité de notre détresse humaine
Et tant mieux si votre altitude ouvre la porte aux avalanches!

C'est l'heure où le boiteux ne croit plus à sa boiterie,
Où le paralytique se dégage avec calme
De son torrent à sec, de pierre et de cailloux,
Et le poète soupèse le glissant soleil
Avec les paumes de ses mains qui s'acheminent vers l'esprit pur,
Et le vin de l'univers saute à la tête de l'homme
Qui, enjambant tous les obstacles, se mesure avec l'univers.
Sa personnelle lumière enfourche la cavalerie du soleil.
Tous ces sabots en même temps martèlent une moitié de la terre,
L'autre moitié est dans la nuit où se façonnent et déjà conspirent
De sombres soleils en tournoyante formation.

O moutons sur la colline, ô tigres dans les fourrés,
C'est maintenant que vous allez être moutons et tigres véritables,
Et prendrez d'un seul coup possession de tous vos muscles,
Vous qui n'étiez jusqu'ici que des images coloriées

CONFIDENCE

Powerful mountains, while there is still time
Let us, with eyes wide open, defy the world at your feet
With all the authority born of human distress
And so much the better if your heights throw open the gateway
*   to avalanches!*

It is now that the lame man no longer believes in his lameness,
Now, that the paralytic calmly breaks free
From his dried-up torrent of pebbles and stones,
And the poet weighs the slippery sun
In the palms of his hands as they pass towards pure spirit,
And the wine of the universe leaps to the head of the man
Who, stepping over all obstacles, pits himself against the universe.
His personal light bestrides the cavalry of the sun.
All those hoofs at once are hammering half the earth,
The other half is plunged in a night where somber suns in whirling
*   formation*
Are fashioned and already conspire.

O sheep on the hill, tigers in the thickets,
It is now you are going to be sheep and tigers for real,
Taking instant possession of all your muscles,
You that till now were only colored pictures

--C'était tout plat dans l'attente du mouvement et du souffle--
Voilà que soudain mûris par la sève nourricière
Vous désertez l'anonymat et pleins de personnalité
Vous remplissez votre peau prêts à la faire éclater,
Vous dégagez à l'envi une lumière de phosphore
Et dans un bruit de pierreries vous vous mettez en mouvement.
Tous les tigres et les moutons qui auraient voulu vivre dans le monde
Et sont restés à l'état de lavis qui s'interrogent
Alimentent votre élan
Dans le ruissellement des choses créés et déjà barbues de puissance
Comme un bélier libéré des entraves du tondeur
Qui se déclenche dans l'air sous le ressort de ses reins
Et bondit avec sa tête toute neuve bien en avant!

--Flat and insipid, waiting for movement and breath--
Now suddenly ripening, fed by the rising sap
You forsake anonymity and full of personality
Fill out your hides, ready to make them burst,
You vie at emitting a phosphorescent light
And to a tinkling of gems and bright stones, begin to move.
All the tigers and sheep who longed to live in the world
And remained mere washes and sketches questioning themselves
Feed your élan
In the streaming torrent of things created and already bearded
  with power
Like a ram freed of the shearer's shackles
Propelling itself into the air by the coilspring of its back
And bounding with head brand-new thrust forward!

LE GALOP SOUTERRAIN

THE UNDERGROUND GALLOP

LE GALOP SOUTERRAIN

Charles Martel où allons-nous
Ainsi dans ce monde sans hommes,
Entourés par des rois de France
Avec leur plus belle couronne?
--Et toi, Prince-des-Noirs-Tableaux
Ne sais-tu pas où nous allons?
Demande au voisin Charles VI
Ou à l'autre, le Téméraire,
Moi je ne puis te renseigner,
Depuis le temps que nos chevaux
Qui n'ont plus besoin de litière
Ni de souffler sur notre route,
Nous entraînent sous cette terre,
Comment veux-tu que je comprenne
Le but de ce cruel voyage
Avec la terre dans la bouche
Avec partout sur notre corps
Des éclaboussures de boue.
--Charles Martel est-ce bien toi
Cette figure qui galope?
Es-tu derrière ou devant moi
A ma droite ou bien à ma gauche?
J'entends ton épée et ton heaume,

THE UNDERGROUND GALLOP

Where are we going Charles Martel
Like this in this world without men
Surrounded by kings of France
Sporting their finest crowns?
--And you there, Prince-of-the-Black-Tableaux
Where we are going, don't you know?
Ask my neighbor Charles the Sixth
Or ask the other Charles, the Bold,
As for myself, I cannot say,
Not since the day our galloping steeds
No longer in need of straw or hay
Or snorting and snuffing along the road
Began dragging us on beneath this earth,
How expect me to understand
The point of this cruel trip
With our mouths all choked with dirt
And our bodies from tip to toe
Splattered and smeared with mud and mire.
--Charles Martel is it really you
That galloping figure in the dark?
Are you behind or in front of me
To my right, to my left? I cannot see.
I hear your sword and your helmet clang,

Dis que tu reconnais ma voix.
(Ici il y eut un silence.)
Charles Martel qu'as-tu donc fait
De ton martel et de ta langue
Puisque tu ne sais plus répondre
A mes demandes raisonnables?
Dis un mot à ton vieil ami
Ah! je ne peux même suivre
Ni ton cheval ni ton silence
Ni même en moi ton souvenir.
--C'est ce qu'il faut, le bon chemin
C'est d'avancer toujours plus vite
Sur la crinière du destin
Et sans jamais demander rien
De ce que sera notre gîte.
Il semble bien que notre troupe
S'accroisse d'autres cavaliers,
Qu'ils suivent, toujours plus nombreux,
Comme de sombres alliés.
--Dis donc n'as-tu pas remarqué
Qu'ils font un drôle de silence
Et qu'on n'entend pas davantage
Leur galopade que la nôtre?
--Il s'agit bien de remarquer,
L'essentiel est d'être nombreux
Pour moins sentir notre terreur
De la mortelle chevauchée.
--Nous approchons, ça sent la viande
Que l'on grille pour le retour
Ça sent le poulet sur la broche.
--Hé non! ça ne sent rien du tout.
--Je te dis que ça sent la femme
Qui va se mettre dans mon lit.

Say that you recognize my voice.
(Here was a voiceless pause.)
Charles Martel what have you done
With your hammer and with your tongue
Since you're unable to reply
To these few reasonable requests?
Just say a word to your old friend.
I can't keep up with you anymore--
Not with your silence, not with your horse
Nor even your memory in me.
--That's what we need, the only way
Is to advance, advance, advance
(Bent over the mane of destiny)
Faster and faster and never ask
To know where our resting-place will be.
Look, it appears our galloping troop
Is growing, other horsemen come,
Let them follow, from more to more,
Like somber allies, swift and dumb.
--Say haven't you noticed, I did now,
The funny silences they make?
Strain as you will, you cannot hear
Their galloping any more than ours.
--Notice? hell! that's hardly the point
The main thing is that our number grow
So we are less aware of our dread
Of the deadly cavalcade.
--We're getting close, it smells of the meat
They're grilling now for the great return
It smells of chicken on the spit.
--Hell no! it smells of nothing at all.
--I tell you it smells of woman, yes
The woman about to slip into my bed.

--Je te dis que nous chevauchons
Et qu'il n'est plus question de femmes.
Nous galopons dans un trou noir
Qui nous surveille aux entournures
Sans permettre le moindre écart.
--Ça sent le faisan qu'on rôtit
Ça sent la pomme que l'on cuit.
--Mon pauvre ami, laisse-moi rire
Toi qui n'as même plus de nez!
Ce qui t'en reste déraisonne
D'être ainsi rogné jusqu'à l'os.
--Regarde-moi de tes deux yeux
Afin que je sache où j'en suis.
--Ne me parle pas de nos yeux
Ni de nos coeurs dans nos poitrines,
Ce sont des souvenirs sans chair
Ils agrandissent ce désert.
--Alors que veux-tu que je dise
Si tous les mots sont interdits
Ou s'ils ne s'offrent à l'esprit
Que terrassés par leurs contraires?
--Il nous reste encor *galoper*
Tirons-en le meilleur parti.

1938.

--I tell you, my friend, we are riding hard
And nobody's talking of women now.
We're galloping hard in a pitch-black pit
Which eyes us as from the top of a sleeve
And won't allow us to swerve or slip.
--It smells of pheasant they're roasting, I'd swear
It smells of apples they're baking there.
--My poor old friend, don't make me laugh,
Who told you you had a nose anymore!
All you have left spouts arrant nonsense
Pared off as it is right down to the bone.
--Look at me, stare me straight in the eyes
So I can see just how I stand.
--Don't talk to me about our eyes,
Forget our hearts in our hollow chests,
They're fleshless memories at best
And make this desert wider yet.
--Well, then what do you want me to say
If every word I propose is banned
Or only leaps to mind
Tripped up by its opposite?
--All we can do is *gallop, gallop*
Let's make the best of it we can.

1938.

73

EN SONGEANT
A UN ART POÉTIQUE

THOUGHTS TOWARD
AN ARS POETICA

La poésie vient chez moi d'un rêve toujours latent. Ce rêve j'aime à le diriger, sauf les jours d'inspiration où j'ai l'impression qu'il se dirige tout seul.

Je n'aime pas le rêve qui s'en va à la dérive (j'allais dire à la dérêve). Je cherche à en faire un rêve consistant, une sorte de figure de proue qui après avoir traversé les espaces et le temps intérieurs affronte les espaces et le temps du dehors--et pour lui le dehors c'est la page blanche.

Rêver, c'est oublier la matérialité de son corps, confondre en quelque sorte le monde extérieur et l'intérieur. L'omniprésence du poète cosmique n'a peut-être pas d'autre origine. Je rêve toujours un peu ce que je vois, même au moment précis et au fur et à mesure que je le vois, et ce que j'éprouvais dans "Boire à la Source" est toujours vrai: quand je vais dans la campagne le paysage me devient presque tout de suite intérieur par je ne sais quel glissement du dehors vers le dedans, j'avance comme dans mon propre monde mental.

On s'est parfois étonné de mon émerveillement devant le monde, il me vient autant de la permanence du rêve que de ma mauvaise mémoire. Tous deux me font aller de surprise en surprise et me forcent encore à m'étonner de tout. "Tiens, il y a des arbres, il y a la mer. Il y a des femmes. Il en est même de fort belles . . . ."

Poetry, for me, comes from a latent dream, always there, just below the surface. It is a dream I like to guide, except on days of inspiration when it seems to guide itself.

I am not fond of the dream that goes adrift (I was about to say "a-dream"). I try to make of it a consistent dream, a sort of ship's figurehead which, after having journeyed through inner space and time, confronts space and time outside--and for it, this outside is the blank page.

To dream is to forget the material existence of the body, to confuse, in a way, the outer and the inner worlds. The cosmic poet's feeling of omnipresence has perhaps no other origin. I always tend to dream what I see, even at the very moment I am seeing it, and the experience I described in *Boire à la Source* (*Drink at the Source*) is still true: when I walk in the country, the landscape almost at once becomes part of me, slipping mysteriously from the outside toward the inside, I advance, as it were, in my own mental world.

People have at times been astonished by my perpetual state of wonderment in the presence of the world; that comes no less from this permanence of the dream-state in me than from my poor memory. Both lead me on from surprise to surprise and compel me to marvel at everything. "Look! there are trees, there is the sea. There are women. Very beautiful ones even. . . ."

77

Mais si je rêve je n'en suis pas moins attiré en poésie par une grande précision, par une sorte d'exactitude hallucinée. N'est-ce pas justement ainsi que se manifeste le rêve du dormeur? Il est parfaitement défini même dans ses ambiguïtés. C'est au réveil que les contours s'effacent et que le rêve devient flou, inconsistant.

Si je me suis révélé assez tard, c'est que longtemps j'ai éludé mon moi profond. Je n'osais pas l'affronter directement et ce furent les "Poèmes de l'humour triste". Il me fallut avoir les nerfs assez solides pour faire face aux vertiges, aux traquenards du cosmos intérieur dont j'ai toujours le sentiment très vif et comme cénesthésique.

J'ai été long à venir à la poésie moderne, à être attiré par Rimbaud et Apollinaire. Je ne parvenais pas à franchir les murs de flammes et de fumée qui séparent ces poètes des classiques, des romantiques. Et s'il m'est permis de faire un aveu, lequel n'est peut-être qu'un souhait, j'ai tenté par la suite d'être un de ceux qui dissipèrent cette fumée en tâchant de ne pas éteindre la flamme, un conciliateur, un réconciliateur des poésies ancienne et moderne.

Alors que la poésie s'était bien déshumanisée, je me suis proposé, dans la continuité et la lumière chères aux classiques, de faire sentir les tourments, les espoirs et les angoisses d'un poète et d'un homme d'aujourd'hui. Je songe à certaine préface, à peu près inconnue, de Valéry à un jeune poète: "Ne soyez pas mécontent de vos vers, disait le poète de *Charmes* à André Caselli. Je leur ai trouvé d'exquises qualités dont l'une est essentielle pour mon goût, je veux parler d'une sincérité dans l'accent qui est pour le poète l'analogue de la justesse de voix chez les chanteurs. Gardez ce ton *réel*. Ne vous étonnez pas que ce soit moi qui le remarque dans vos poèmes et qui le loue. Mais voici l'immense difficulté. Elle est de combiner ce son juste de l'âme avec l'artifice de l'art. Il faut énormément d'art pour

But although I dream, I am nonetheless attracted by clarity and precision in poetry, by a sort of hallucinatory exactness and attention to detail. Is it not in just this way that the dream of the sleeper manifests itself? It is clearly defined in all its ambiguity. Only when we awake do the contours fade and the dream becomes blurred, inconsistent.

If I found myself rather late in life, it is because for a long time I eluded the deeper me. I dared not confront it directly, and the result was the *Poèmes de l'humour triste* (*Poems of Melancholy Humor*). I needed to develop nerves solid enough to face the vertigoes, the pitfalls of my inner cosmos, of which I have always been very keenly and, as it were, cenesthetically aware.

I took a long time coming to modern poetry, a long time before I was attracted by Rimbaud and Apollinaire. I was unable to leap the walls of flame and smoke which separate these poets from the classic, the romantic poets. And if I may make a confession, which is perhaps only a wish or a hope, I have tried, since then, to be one of those who cleared away the smoke while trying not to put out the flame, a conciliator, a reconciler of traditional and modern poetry.

At a time when poetry had become more than a little dehumanized, I set myself the task, in the enlightened tradition dear to our classic writers, of expressing the torments, the hopes and the anguish of a poet and man living today. I am reminded of an all but unknown preface written by Valéry for a young poet. "Do not be dissatisfied with your poems," said the poet of *Charmes* to André Caselli. "In them I have found exquisite qualities--one of which, to my sense of taste, is essential: I am referring to a certain sincerity of tone, which, for the poet, is the equivalent of true pitch for singers. Keep that true, that *genuine* tone. Do not be surprised I should be the one to notice it in your poems and to praise it. But here is the immense difficulty: to combine this

être véritablement soi-même et simple. Mais l'art tout seul ne saurait suffire."

Ce ton réel, cette sincérité dans l'accent, cette simplicité, j'ai toujours tâché pour mon compte de les retenir: elles étaient en moi suffisamment submergées dans le rêve pour ne pas nuire à la poésie. On a fait de notre temps une telle consommation de folie en vers et en prose que cette folie n'a plus pour moi de vertu apéritive et je trouve bien plus de piment et même de moutarde dans une certaine sagesse gouvernant cette folie et lui donnant l'apparence de la raison que dans le délire livré à lui-même.

Il y a certes une part de délire dans toute création poétique mais ce délire doit être décanté, séparé des résidus inopérants ou nuisibles, avec toutes les précautions que comporte cette opération délicate. Pour moi ce n'est qu'à force de simplicité et de transparence que je parviens à aborder mes secrets essentiels et à décanter ma poésie profonde. Tendre à ce que le surnaturel devienne naturel et coule de source (ou en ait l'air). Faire en sorte que l'ineffable nous devienne familier tout en gardant ses racines fabuleuses.

Le poète dispose de deux pédales, la claire lui permet d'aller jusqu'à la transparence, l'obscure va jusqu'à l'opacité. Je crois n'avoir que rarement appuyé sur la pédale obscure. Si je voile c'est naturellement et ce n'est là, je le voudrais, que le voile de la poésie. Le poète opère souvent à chaud dans les ténèbres mais l'opération à froid a aussi ses avantages. Elle nous permet des audaces plus grandes parce que plus lucides. Nous savons que nous n'aurons pas à en rougir un jour comme d'une ivresse passagère et de certains emportements que nous ne comprenons plus. J'ai d'autant plus besoin de cette lucidité que je suis naturellement obscur. Il n'est pas de poésie pour moi sans une certaine confusion au départ. Je tâche d'y mettre des lumières sans faire perdre sa vitalité à l'inconscient.

true tone of the soul with the artifice of art. One needs an extraordinary amount of art to be truly oneself and simple. But art alone is never enough."

This genuine tone, this sincerity of accent, this simplicity, I, for my part, have always tried to retain: in me they were sufficiently submerged in dream not to work against the poetry. In our time, we have indulged in such a glut of extravagance, of folly in verse and prose that my appetite is no longer stimulated by it. I find much more spice and even mustard in a certain *sagesse* [sensible moderation] governing this folly and lending it a semblance of reason than in delirium left to its own devices.

There is certainly an element of delirium in any act of poetic creation but this delirium must be decanted, separated out from the inoperative and noxious residue, with all the precautions such a delicate process entails. As for me, it is only by dint of simplicity and transparency that I manage to make contact with my essential secrets and decant my deepest poetry. Strive to let the supernatural become natural and flow freely (or seem to). Let the ineffable become familiar, all the while keeping its fabulous, its mythical roots.

The poet has two pedals at his disposal--the one, clear, allows him to attain transparency, the other, obscure, may be pushed all the way to opaqueness. I have, I believe, only rarely stepped on the pedal of the obscure. If I interpose a veil, it is done naturally, without thinking, and it is, I should hope, only the veil of poetry. The poet often operates in the dark under extreme pressure, but a cool-headed, calculated operation also has its advantages. It permits innovations that are more daring because more lucid. We know they will not, one day, give us cause to blush, as might some temporary intoxication and certain fits of anger we are later at a loss to explain. I need lucidity--all the more so because I am by nature obscure. No poetry comes to me without an element

Je n'aime l'étrange que s'il est acclimaté, amené à la température humaine. Je m'essaie à faire une ligne droite avec une ou plusieurs lignes brisées. Certains poètes sont souvent victimes de leurs transes. Ils se laissent aller au seul plaisir de se délivrer et ne s'inquiètent nullement de la beauté du poème. Ou pour me servir d'une autre image ils remplissent leur verre à ras bord et oublient de vous servir, vous, lecteur.

Je n'ai guère connu la peur de la banalité qui hante la plupart des écrivains mais bien plutôt celle de l'incompréhension et de la singularité. N'écrivant pas pour des spécialistes du mystère j'ai toujours souffert quand une personne sensible ne comprenait pas un de mes poèmes.

L'image est la lanterne magique qui éclaire les poètes dans l'obscurité. Elle est aussi la surface éclairée lorsqu'il s'approche de ce centre mystérieux où bat le coeur même de la poésie. Mais il n'y a pas que les images. Il y a les passages des unes aux autres qui doivent être aussi de la poésie. Quant à l'explication, on a dit qu'elle était antipoétique et c'est vrai s'il s'agit d'une explication telle que l'entendent les logiciens. Mais il en est de submergées dans le rêve qui peuvent se manifester sans sortir de la poésie.

Ainsi le poète peut aspirer à la cohérence, à la plausibilité de tout le poème dont la surface sera limpide alors que le mystère se réfugiera dans les profondeurs. Je compte sur mon poème pour ordonner et faire chanter juste les images. Comme il baigne chez moi dans le rêve intérieur je ne crains pas de lui faire prendre parfois la forme d'un récit. La logique du conteur surveille la rêverie divagante du poète. La cohésion de tout le poème loin d'en détruire la magie en consolide les assises. Et quand je dis que le conteur surveille en moi le poète je ne perds pas de vue, bien sûr, les différences entre les genres littéraires. Le conte va

of confusion at the start. I try to fill it with points of light without causing the unconscious to lose its vitality.

I like what is strange only when it is acclimated, brought up to human temperature. I work at making a straight line out of one or several broken lines. Certain poets are frequently victims of their own trances. They surrender to the sheer pleasure of unburdening themselves and are totally unconcerned with beauty. Or, to use another image, they fill their glasses to the brim and forget to serve you, the reader.

I have never really known that fear of banality, of unoriginality which haunts most writers, but the fear, rather, of incomprehensibility and peculiarity. Since I do not write for mystery specialists, I have always suffered when a sensitive person did not understand one of my poems.

The image is the magic lantern which lights and guides the poet in the dark. And it is the illuminated surface when he approaches that mysterious center where the very heart of poetry beats. But images are just part of the poem. There are the passages connecting one image to another, and they too must be poetry. As for explanations, they have been called unpoetic--which is true, if we are thinking of explanations as a logician might. But there are explanations which, submerged in dream, may express themselves without departing from the domain of poetry.

Thus the poet can aspire to achieve coherence and plausibility in the entire poem, the surface of which will remain limpid even as mystery takes refuge in its depths. I count upon my poem to arrange its images in proper order and to make them sing true. Since it is bathed in my inner dream-world, I am not afraid to let it occasionally take on narrative form. The logic of the storyteller monitors the shifting reverie of the poet. The coherence, the consistency of the entire poem, far from destroying its magic, consolidates its foundations. And when I say that the storyteller

directement d'un point à un autre alors que le poème, tel que je le conçois généralement, avance en cercles concentriques.

Je suis d'une famille de petits horlogers qui ont travaillé, leur vie durant, la loupe vissée à l'oeil. Les moindres petits ressorts doivent être à leur place si l'on veut que tout le poème se mette en mouvement sous nos yeux.

Je n'attends pas l'inspiration pour écrire et je fais à sa rencontre plus de la moitié du chemin. Le poète ne peut compter sur les moments très rares où il écrit comme sous une dictée. Et il me semble qu'il doit imiter en cela l'homme de science lequel n'attend pas d'être inspiré pour se mettre au travail. La science est en cela une excellente école de modestie à moins que ce ne soit du contraire puisqu'elle fait confiance à la valeur constante de l'homme et non pas seulement à quelques moments privilégiés. Que de fois nous pensons n'avoir rien à dire alors qu'un poème attend en nous derrière un mince rideau de brume et il suffit de faire taire le bruit des contingences pour que ce poème se dévoile à nous.

Stendhal ne croyait qu'à l'opiniâtreté chez l'écrivain. Je pense qu'il songeait aussi à cette opiniâtreté involontaire qui est le fruit d'une longue obsession. Parfois ce qu'on nomme l'inspiration vient de ce que le poète bénéficie d'une opiniâtreté inconsciente et *ancienne* qui finit un jour par porter ses fruits. Elle nous permet de voir en nous comme par une lucarne ce qui est invisible en temps ordinaire.

Je n'aime pas l'originalité trop singulière (à part quelques radieuses exceptions comme, en France, Lautréamont ou Michaux), je préfère une originalité moins consciente comme chez nos classiques.

Malgré les merveilleux exemples de certains poètes qui transforment les mots en objets précieux, j'écris souvent sans penser aux mots, je m'efforce même d'oublier leur existence pour cerner de plus en plus étroitement ma pensée ou plutôt

in me monitors the poet, I am, of course, not losing sight of the differences between literary genres. A story proceeds directly from point to point, whereas the poem, as I generally conceive of it, advances in concentric circles.

I come from a family of humble watchmakers who worked their whole life long, eyes glued to a magnifying glass. The least little springs and wheels must be in place for the poem to set itself in motion, as we watch.

I do not wait for inspiration before starting to write, and I go out to meet it more than half-way. The poet cannot count on those very rare moments when he writes as if taking down dictation. And in this respect he must, I think, imitate the scientist, who does not wait to be inspired before setting to work. Science is, in this matter, an excellent school of modesty--unless it is just the opposite--for it has faith in the constant value of man--a value not limited to a few privileged moments. How often we think we have nothing to say, when, in reality, a poem is waiting inside us behind a thin curtain of mist, and we have only to shut out the noise of everyday event for the poem to be revealed.

In the writer, Stendhal trusted only in obstinacy. I believe he may also have been thinking of that involuntary obstinacy which is the fruit of a long obsession. Sometimes what we call inspiration is simply the poet's benefiting from an unconscious and *inveterate* obstinacy which finally bears fruit. An obstinacy which allows us to look inside as through a skylight and see things that are not visible on ordinary days.

I do not care for an overly idiosyncratic kind of originality (aside from a few radiant exceptions like, in France, Lautréamont or Michaux); I prefer an originality which is less self-conscious, as with our classic writers.

Despite the marvelous examples furnished by certain poets, who transform words into precious objects, I often write without giving a thought to my words; I even make an effort

cet état intermédiaire entre la pensée et le rêve qui donne naissance au poème. Il ne s'agit pas en effet de penser à proprement parler en poésie mais d'en donner en quelque sorte l'équivalent ou la nostalgie. Le sentiment de la création, du moins tel que j'ai pu l'éprouver, j'ai tenté de le montrer dans la page qui suit, en réponse à une enquête de Jean Paulhan à la N.R.F. (Mais c'est là un état d'ivresse lyrique que j'ai rarement ressentie dans sa plénitude et on a vu par les pages qui précèdent que je n'attends pas pour écrire cet état de transe.) "L'inspiration se manifeste en général chez moi par le sentiment que je suis partout à la fois, aussi bien dans l'espace que dans les diverses régions du coeur et de la pensée. L'état de poésie me vient alors d'une sorte de confusion magique où les idées et les images se mettent à vivre, abandonnent leurs arêtes, soit pour faire des avances à d'autres images--dans ce domaine tout voisine, rien n'est vraiment éloigné--soit pour subir de profondes métamorphoses qui les rendent méconnaissables. Cependant pour l'esprit, mélangé de rêves, les contraires n'existent plus: l'affirmation et la négation deviennent une même chose et aussi le passé et l'avenir, le désespoir et l'espérance, la folie et la raison, la mort et la vie. Le chant intérieur s'élève, il choisit les mots qui lui conviennent. Je me donne l'illusion de seconder l'obscur dans son effort vers la lumière pendant qu'affleurent à la surface du papier les images qui bougeaient, réclamant dans les profondeurs. Après quoi je sais un peu mieux où j'en suis de moi-même, j'ai créé de dangereuses puissances et je les ai exorcisées, j'en ai fait des alliés de ma raison la plus intérieure."

Paulhan me disait que mon exposé tournait au poème en prose. C'est que la plupart du temps je n'avance dans ma pensée qu'à la faveur des images. Si l'image, même quand elle est juste, est plus imprécise que le concept, elle rayonne davantage   et va plus loin dans l'inconscient. Elle l'incarne

to forget they exist, so as to zero in on my thought or, rather, on that intermediate state between thought and dream which gives birth to the poem. In poetry it is not, strictly speaking, a question of thinking, but of producing, as it were, its equivalent, a kind of nostalgia for thought. As for the feelings associated with the act of creation--as I have experienced them at least--I have sought to describe them in the following passage, written in reply to a survey done by Jean Paulhan for the *N.R.F.* (But this is a state of lyric intoxication I have rarely experienced to the full and, as you have seen from the preceding pages, I do not wait for this trance-like state before starting to write.) "Inspiration generally makes itself known to me through the feeling I am everywhere at once, in space as well as in the different regions of the heart and of thought. The poetic state then arises from a sort of magical confusion in which ideas and images start to life, abandoning their fixed structures, either to make advances toward other images--in this domain everything is nearby, nothing is truly remote--or to undergo profound metamorphoses which render them unrecognizable. Meanwhile, for the mind, suffused with dreams, contraries no longer exist: affirmation and negation become identical, as do past and future, despair and hope, madness and reason, death and life. The inner song ascends, it chooses the words that suit its needs. I give myself the illusion of helping the obscure in its effort to reach the light, while the images which were stirring, crying out in the depths, rise to the surface of the paper. After which, I know a little better where I stand. I have created dangerous powers and I have exorcised them, I have made them allies of my innermost reason."

Paulhan used to say that my statement itself tended toward the prose poem. The fact is, most of the time, I move from point to point in my thought only with the help of images. If the image, even when it is exact, is more imprecise than a

dans le poème alors que le concept plus ou moins formulé, n'est là que pour l'intelligibilité et pour permettre au poème d'atteindre une autre image qui émerge peu à peu des profondeurs.

S'il est quelque humanité dans ma poésie c'est peut-être que je cultive mes terres pauvres avec un engrais éprouvé, la souffrance. Et c'est peut-être cette anxiété sourde, continuelle qui empêche souvent ma poésie d'être plus brillante. Souffrir dans son corps ou dans ses idées c'est penser à soi, se retourner contre soi. Penser à soi, malgré soi, c'est être misérable et dépourvu d'ornements. J'ai toujours plus ou moins redouté de m'attaquer aux monstres que je sens en moi. Je préfère les apprivoiser avec les mots de tous les jours, lesquels sont rassurants entre tous. (Ne sont-ils pas ceux-là mêmes qui nous ont tranquillisés lors des grandes peurs enfantines?) Je compte sur leur sagesse et leur amitié maintes fois éprouvées pour neutraliser le venin de l'insolite, souvent précurseur de panique. Et peut-être dois-je le meilleur de ma sagesse à ce que j'ai eu souvent à dompter un peu de folie.

Je n'aime pas en poésie (dans la mienne, du moins) les richesses très apparentes. Je les préfère sourdes et un peu confuses de leur éclat, quand elles en ont. S'il doit se produire, que le miracle s'avance à pas de loup et se retire de même après avoir fait son coup. J'aime à acculer jusqu'au dépouillement les sentiments les plus enchevêtrés et les sensations les plus étranges qui se pressent en nous. Je crois aussi beaucoup en la vertu au sein du poème de certaines phrases de prose (encore faut-il qu'elles soient bien accentuées et soulevées par le rythme). Par leur grand naturel dans un moment tragique elles lui apportent un pathétique extraordinaire. Quand Victor Hugo entend venir "les noirs chevaux de la Mort" il ajoute ces deux vers qui sont de pure prose (mais divinement accentuée et rythmée):

concept, it radiates more intensely and penetrates more deeply into the unconscious. The image embodies the unconscious in the poem, whereas the concept, more or less precisely formulated, is there only for the sake of intelligibility and to allow the poem to reach another image emerging bit by bit from the depths.

If there is some degree of humanity in my poetry, it is perhaps because I cultivate my poor soil with a proven fertilizer: suffering. And it is perhaps this dull, continual anxiety which often prevents my poetry from being more brilliant. To suffer in one's body or mind is to think about oneself, to turn against oneself. To think about oneself, in spite of oneself, is to be wretched, impoverished, unadorned. I have always more or less dreaded attacking the monsters I feel inside me. I prefer taming them with everyday words, words that are especially comforting. (Are these not the very words which reassured us during our childhood terrors?) I count on their tried and true *sagesse* [their quiet moderation] and friendship to neutralize the venom of the strange, the unusual, which is often the forerunner of panic. And perhaps I owe the better part of my *sagesse* [moderation, reasonableness] to the fact that I have often had to tame a touch of madness in myself.

In poetry (in mine at least) I dislike conspicuous richness. I prefer it subdued and somewhat embarrassed by its own showiness--when it is showy. If the miracle is to occur, let it advance stealthily and withdraw in the same way after having made its strike. I like to push to the point of utter simplicity and nakedness the most tangled feelings and the strangest sensations jostling inside us. I also firmly believe in the value, at the heart of the poem, of certain sentences in prose (which, however, must be carefully stressed and borne along by the rhythm). By their great simplicity and naturalness at tragic moments, they give the poem an extraordinary

Je suis comme celui qui s'étant trop hâté
Attend sur le chemin que la voiture passe.

Je me sers de formes poétiques très différentes: vers
réguliers (ou presque), vers blancs qui riment quand la rime
vient à moi, vers libres, versets qui se rapprochent de la prose
rythmée. Aimant par-dessus tout le naturel, je ne me dis
jamais à l'avance que j'emploierai telle ou telle forme. Je
laisse mon poème lui-même faire son choix. Ce n'est pas là
mépris mais assouplissement de la technique. Ou, si l'on
préfère, technique mouvante qui ne se fixe qu'à chaque
poème dont elle épouse le chant. Ce qui peut-être permet
une grande variété d'inspiration.

L'art poétique est pour chaque poète l'éloge plus ou moins
indiscret de la poésie où il excelle. Et c'est ainsi que Verlaine
nous recommande les vers impairs, Valéry les vers réguliers
de forme classique et mallarméenne, Claudel le verset. Qu'on
me pardonne si j'ai exposé mes préférences avec beaucoup
plus de naïveté que mes illustres prédécesseurs et une
nonchalance qui va de pair avec la rêverie. J'aime à écrire
sans trop savoir et de préférence dans un jardin où c'est la
nature qui a l'air de faire tout le travail. Certes le grand air,
les espaces sans murs empêchent un peu la concentration
mais si le jardin est clos ils favorisent la distraction dirigée,
amie de la poésie, des ombrages et de la fraîcheur.

Chaque poète a ses secrets. J'ai essayé de vous dire
quelques-uns des miens en vous dévoilant ce double de
nous-même qui dans l'ombre nous surveille, nous approuve
ou nous fait déchirer la feuille que nous venons d'écrire.
Mais je ne vous ai presque rien dit du plus important de nos
secrets, ce mystère qui habite le poète et dont il ne parvient
jamais à se séparer complètement pour pouvoir, du dehors,
le juger. Puisse-t-il avoir trouvé refuge dans mes poèmes.

pathos. When Victor Hugo hears "the black horses of Death," he adds these two verses, which are pure prose (but divinely stressed and cadenced):

I am like him who, having hastened, waits
Beside the road until the coach has come.

I employ a broad range of poetic forms: traditional verse (or almost), blank verse that rhymes when the rhyme occurs to me, free verse, *versets* [as in the Bible] that are close to cadenced prose. Liking first and foremost what is free and natural, I never tell myself in advance, I'm going to use this or that form. I let my poem make its own choice. This is not out of disregard for technique but rather in the interest of suppleness, flexibility. Or, if you prefer, a shifting technique which settles upon a form in contact with each new poem, whose song it adopts. --Which perhaps allows me a great variety of inspiration.

For every poet, his *ars poetica* is the more or less indiscreet eulogy of the kind of poetry he excels at. And that is why Verlaine recommends *les vers impairs* [verses with an uneven number of syllables], Valéry traditional classical, Mallarméan verse, Claudel the *verset*. May I be excused for stating my preferences with considerably more naïveté than my illustrious predecessors--and a nonchalance that goes hand in hand with reverie. I like to write without being particularly aware of it and preferably in a garden, where nature seems to be doing all the work. To be sure, open air and unwalled spaces somewhat impede total concentration, but if the garden is closed in, they promote a sort of guided distractedness, a friend to poetry, to shade and to coolness.

Every poet has his secrets. I have tried to tell you some of mine by revealing that double of ourselves who, from the shadows, watches over us, approves what we do or makes us

tear up the page we have just written. But I have told you practically nothing of the most important of our secrets, that mystery which inhabits the poet and from which he never succeeds in completely separating himself, so as to judge it from outside. May it have found refuge in my poems.

LIRE DES VERS EN PUBLIC

Ce n'est pas un simple jeu de la vanité pour le poète que de dire ses vers en public. A la projeter ainsi devant soi dans une épreuve redoutable, il n'est pas fâché de sentir si son oeuvre est vraiment transmissible et achevée ou si quelque défaut ne viendra pas se retourner en l'air même, contre lui.

Certes, l'imprimé que l'on suit des yeux, la communion silencieuse et sans intermédiaire du texte muet et du lecteur favorisent une concentration sans égale et d'autant plus précieuse qu'elle s'entrouvre sur une exaltation sans témoins. Mais le vers n'est-il pas fait surtout pour la vie vocale, n'attend-il pas que la voix de l'homme vienne le délivrer des caractères d'imprimerie, de leur poids, leur silence, leur geôle, de leur indifférence apparente?

La voix humaine, si elle est compréhensive, donne au vers un véhicule quasi métaphysique. N'est-elle pas la fusion du corps et de l'esprit, un fluide qui s'évade dans l'air tout en se révélant.

Les jolis gallicismes *savoir par coeur*, *réciter par coeur*, puisqu'il n'est pas de mémoire profonde qui ne passe par là, sont bien de mise en poésie où Ronsard, Racine, Baudelaire, Hugo, Rimbaud, Valéry sont pour quelque chose dans le battement de nos coeurs.

Les vers des poètes classiques se mêlent chaque jour à la vie des hommes par la voix des écoliers.

READING POETRY IN PUBLIC

For a poet to recite his poems in public is no mere exercise in self-indulgence. By projecting his work into the world, by putting it to this terrifying test, he is not dismayed to sense whether it is truly finished and can be communicated, or whether perhaps some imperfection or other may turn back upon him in mid-air.

To be sure, the printed word, followed by the eye, the silent, unmediated communion of mute text and reader, promote an unparalleled level of concentration, all the more precious because it opens out into a state of intensely private exaltation. But poetry is made, is it not?, first and foremost to be spoken, it is waiting for the human voice to deliver it from the weight, the silence, the prison, the seeming indifference of the printer's type.

The human voice, if it is sympathetic, provides verse with an almost metaphysical medium. Is voice not a fusion of body and spirit, a fluid revealing itself even as it escapes into the air.

Those pretty Gallicisms, *know by heart*, *recite by heart*--and all deep memory must take that path--are not out of place in poetry, where Ronsard, Racine, Baudelaire, Hugo, Rimbaud, Valéry count for something in the very beating of our hearts.

Lines from our classic poets daily mingle with the lives of men through the voices of schoolchildren.

Un enfant se lève en classe
Et voici du fond des temps
Que Racine prend sa place
Sur ses lèvres un moment,
Puis c'est Jean de la Fontaine
Qui d'un monde fabuleux
Souffle tout bas son poème
A l'élève studieux.
. . . A combien de neiges, de pluies
A combien de coups de tonnerre
Villon et Ronsard résistèrent
Protégés par leur poésie!
De combien d'émeutes, de guerres
Ne sont-ils pas sortis vivants
Comme lorsqu'ils avaient vingt ans
Et disaient eux-mêmes leurs vers.

Bergson voudrait que l'art de la diction ne fût pas considéré comme un art d'agrément. "Au lieu d'arriver à la fin des études, comme un ornement il devrait être au début et partout, comme un soutien. Sur lui nous poserions tout le reste, si nous ne cédions ici encore à l'illusion que le principal est de discourir sur les choses et qu'on les connaît suffisamment quand on sait en parler. Mais on ne connaît, on ne comprend que ce qu'on peut en quelque mesure réinventer."

Qui dit le poème en public doit donner l'impression de la création à l'état naissant. S'adresser à un auditoire est aussi un efficace remède contre la faveur imméritée d'une poésie opaque, intransmissible, et d'autant plus monotone qu'elle étouffe son propre sens à mesure qu'il tend à se manifester. Poésie chiffrée dont le poète ne connaît pas toujours le chiffre, poésie dont il brouille le chiffre dès qu'il pense le connaître.

A child stands up in class
And out of the depths of time
Racine assumes his place
On his lips and speaks his lines.
Then Jean de la Fontaine
From a world of fable smiles
As he whispers his verses in
The ear of the studious child.
. . . How many snows and rains,
Thunderbolts and worse
Villon and Ronsard withstood
Protected by their verse!
How many riots, wars, hells
Have they emerged from, alive
As when they were twenty-five
And spoke their poems themselves.

Bergson would like to see the art of diction regarded as
something more than a mere social accomplishment. "In-
stead of coming at the end of our studies, a sort of
embellishment, it should be placed at the very beginning--and
at every stage--as a stay and support. On it we would build
all the rest, did we not succumb to the illusion, here as else-
where, that what is important is to be able to hold forth on
a variety of topics and that we are adequately acquainted
with them when we know how to talk about them. But we
know--we understand--only what we can, to some degree, re-
invent."

The person who recites a poem in public must create the
impression of life leaping into existence before our very eyes.
The act of communicating with an audience is also an effec-
tive remedy for the undeserved favor enjoyed by opaque po-
etry, a poetry which cannot be transmitted and which is all

Et pourtant tout ce qui est interdit au poète dans la vie, lui devient possible et même recommandable dans une poésie transparente. . . Il lui suffit des mots qu'il a dans la tête pour s'offrir des palais, des parfums, des femmes, des festins. La poésie est pour les poètes l'art de ne se priver de rien et, par cela même, de nous combler de tout. Ils en arrivent à se prendre pour le Créateur et le comble est qu'ils n'ont pas tout à fait tort puisqu'on retrouve dans leur univers toutes les bêtes du paradis terrestre voisinant avec quelques monstres qui leur sont particuliers.

Les non-poètes oublient le fardeau vital dans leurs diverses occupations, mais ses occupations à lui poète, Atlas de la souffrance humaine, c'est justement de se souvenir de son fardeau. Pour l'alléger il le chante et "l'enchante", comme dirait Albert Béguin. Et même si on écrit une poésie dépouillée, ce n'est jamais tout à fait à nu qu'on nous livre sa détresse. Le vers, même humble, est sur le chemin de la richesse. La seule étoile du Desdichado est morte mais son luth n'en est pas moins constellé.

the more monotonous because it stifles its own meaning even as that meaning tends to unfold. A coded poetry whose code the poet does not always know, a poetry whose code he scrambles as soon as he thinks he knows it.

And yet everything forbidden the poet in life becomes possible and even desirable in transparent poetry. All he needs are the words in his head: he can treat himself to palaces, perfumes, women, revelry. For poets, poetry is the art of denying oneself nothing and, thereby, giving us everything in full measure. They come to take themselves for God the Creator, and the fact is, they are not altogether wrong, for in their universes we find all the creatures of the Garden of Eden side by side with a few monsters of their own making.

Non-poets forget life's burden amid their varied occupations, but the occupation of the poet, Atlas of human suffering, is just that: to remember his burden. To ease it, he chants it, "enchants it," as Albert Béguin might say. And even if he writes a plain, unadorned kind of poetry, it is never in utter nakedness that he tells us of his distress. Poetry, even when humble, is on the road to riches. The single star of the Desdichado is dead but his lute is no less studded with stars.

Acknowledgment

In earlier, slightly different versions, the poems "Insomnia" and "Pure Child" (under the titles "Sleepless" and "This Pure Child") appeared in *Graham House Review* (Colgate University Press), vol. 9, Fall 1985.

Acknowledgment is made to the editors for permission to reprint.

𝔖cripta 𝔥umanistica®

Directed by
BRUNO M. DAMIANI
The Catholic University of America
COMPREHENSIVE LIST OF PUBLICATIONS *

1. Everett W. Hesse, *The "Comedia" and Points of View.* $24.50
2. Marta Ana Diz, *Patronio y Lucanor: la lectura inteligente "en el tiempo que es turbio."* Prólogo de John Esten Keller. $26.00
3. James F. Jones, Jr., *The Story of a Fair Greek of Yesteryear.* A Translation from the French of Antoine-François Prévost's *L'Histoire d'une Grecque moderne.* With Introduction and Selected Bibliography. $30.00
4. Colette H. Winn, *Jean de Sponde: Les sonnets de la mort ou La Poétique de l'accoutumance.* Préface par Frédéric Deloffre. $22.50
5. Jack Weiner, *"En busca de la justicia social: estudio sobre el teatro español del Siglo de Oro."* $24.50
6. Paul A. Gaeng, *Collapse and Reorganization of the Latin Nominal Flection as Reflected in Epigraphic Sources.* Written with the assistance of Jeffrey T. Chamberlin. $24.00
7. Edna Aizenberg, *The Aleph Weaver: Biblical, Kabbalistic, and Judaic Elements in Borges.* $25.00
8. Michael G. Paulson and Tamara Alvarez-Detrell, *Cervantes, Hardy, and "La fuerza de la sangre."* $25.50
9. Rouben Charles Cholakian, *Deflection/Reflection in the Lyric Poetry of Charles d'Orléans: A Psychosemiotic Reading.* $25.00
10. Kent P. Ljungquist, *The Grand and the Fair: Poe's Landscape Aesthetics and Pictorial Techniques.* $27.50
11. D.W. McPheeters, *Estudios humanísticos sobre la "Celestina."* $20.00
12. Vittorio Felaco, *The Poetry and Selected Prose of Camillo Sbarbaro.* Edited and Translated by Vittorio Felaco. With a Preface by Franco Fido. $25.00
13. María del C. Candau de Cevallos, *Historia de la lengua española.* $33.00
14. *Renaissance and Golden Age Studies in Honor of D.W. McPheeters.* Ed. Bruno M. Damiani. $30.00
15. Bernardo Antonio González, *Parábolas de identidad: Realidad interior y estrategia narrativa en tres novelistas de posguerra.* $28.00
16. Carmelo Gariano, *La Edad Media (Aproximación Alfonsina).* $30.00
17. Gabriella Ibieta, *Tradition and Renewal in "La gloria de don Ramiro".* $27.50
18. *Estudios literarios en honor de Gustavo Correa.* Eds. Charles Faulhaber, Richard Kinkade, T.A. Perry. Preface by Manuel Durán. $25.00
19. George Yost, *Pieracci and Shelly: An Italian Ur-Cenci.* $27.50

BOOK ORDERS

* Clothbound. *All book orders*, except library orders, must be prepaid and addressed to **Scripta Humanistica**, 1383 Kersey Lane, Potomac, Maryland 20854. *Manuscripts* to be considered for publication should be sent to the same address.